HOW I WEATHERED THE STORM OF DIVORCE

~Wise·Bold·True~

WRITTEN BY
LaVon Dormeyer

ILLUSTRATED BY
Kurt Deppenschmidt

For Use With Children Ages 7~12

❖ DEDICATION ❖

For two Mikes, one Skidge, and my special Cyclones.

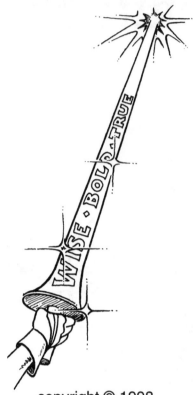

copyright © 1998
mar*co products, inc.

Published by
mar*co products, inc.
1443 Old York Road
Warminster, PA 18974
1-800-448-2197

Library of Congress Catalog Card Number: 98-67898

ISBN: 1-57543-064-9

Printed in the U.S.A.

✥ CONTENTS ✥

A MESSAGE FROM LAVON DORMEYER 5

INTRODUCTION 7

GROUP FACILITATOR'S GUIDE/PRE-GROUP PREPARATION 8

PERMISSION LETTER 9

SESSION 1 10

SESSION 2 12

SESSION 3 14

SESSION 4 16

SESSION 5 18

SESSION 6 20

SESSION 7 22

SESSION 8 24

SESSION 9 26

REPRODUCIBLE BOOKLET .... IMMEDIATELY FOLLOWING SESSIONS

✠ A MESSAGE FROM LAVON DORMEYER ✠

When one of my high-school teachers told me I'd go far, I thought he was speaking figuratively. As it turned out, I married an Army officer shortly after graduating from the University of Utah, and have been on the go ever since. During this time, I have lived in Europe, Australia, and throughout the United States. Although military life makes it difficult to establish a career, I have been richly rewarded with opportunities in teaching adults and children, soldiers, refugees, and civilians. In 1986, I earned my Masters Degree in counseling from Murray State University. Shortly thereafter, we were transferred to my husband's home state, Florida, where I began working as an elementary guidance counselor for Pasco County Schools. In 1995, I became the first guidance counselor to be named Pasco District's Teacher of the Year, a title that I owe in large part to my alter ego, Rose Blossom, who teaches primary students all about sowing seeds of kindness. My love for children and animals has resulted in my having been involved in a number of zoo-outreach programs, my favorite of which are the educational programs I conduct for the Florida Bat Center. I am the "batty" mother of two stupendous sons, Michael and Piers, and the "adoptive" mom of Louis Lizard; Storm, the dog; Sam and Twinkie, both cats. My husband is a saint.

⚜ INTRODUCTION ⚜

For an ever-increasing number of children, separation and divorce have become a devastating reality with long-term consequences. According to a 1992 report published by the Office of Policy and Planning in Washington, D.C., the number of children who must cope with divorce has more than quadrupled since 1950. Each year since 1972, more than one million children have experienced the upheaval of divorce. Unfortunately, many of these children will face economic hardships as well as emotional problems that may interfere with their cognitive and social development.

Elementary-school-age children face grave emotional concerns brought on by grief, fear, disorganization, yearning for the absent parent, inhibitions of aggression towards parents, anger, conflicts of loyalty, guilt, and unrealistic expectations about their ability to reunite their parents. The pain of divorce cannot be eliminated, but caring adults can help children develop positive coping skills that emphasize problem-solving and changing the way they think about what has happened. *How I Weathered the Storm of Divorce* is designed to provide children ages 7-12 with the opportunity to interact with an adult and create their own stories as they confront the emotional issues associated with the dissolution of the family and, at the same time, learn to understand how to manage negative thoughts, feelings, and actions.

PRE-GROUP PREPARATION:

Reproduce a permission letter (page 9) for each child to give to his/her parent(s).

Reproduce the booklet *How I Weathered the Storm of Divorce* for each child. Give the children only the pages to be used during a particular session. At the conclusion of the final session, the children will put all the pages together and assemble their booklets.

Obtain a manila file folder for each child.

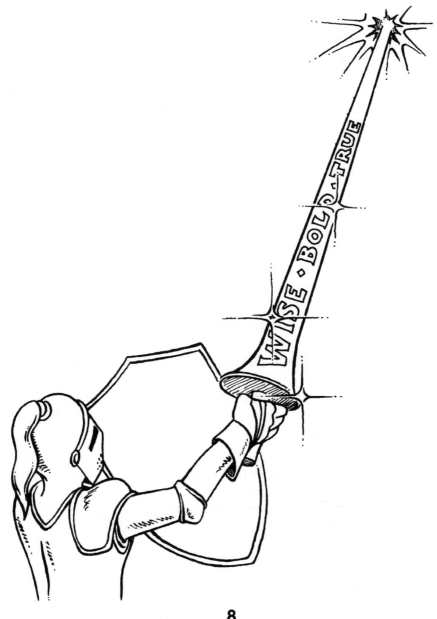

Dear_____ ,

A nine-session group of about _____ children is going to meet to discuss divorce. During the meetings, the children will have an opportunity to share their feelings about divorce and learn how other children feel about the topic. The children will be compiling a booklet entitled *How I Weathered the Storm of Divorce,* which they will be able to bring home after the group has ended.

Be assured that confidentiality will be continually stressed throughout the sessions.

Please indicate your decision concerning your child's participation in the group and return the bottom portion of this letter to _____ by _____ .

Sincerely,

_____

✂ -

☐ **YES,** I will allow my child to participate in the small group on divorce.

☐ **NO,** I prefer my child to does not participate in the small group on divorce.

Child's name _____
Parent's signature _____
Date _____

⚔ SESSION 1 ⚔

MATERIALS NEEDED:

- **For each child:** Copy of page 2 from *How I Weathered the Storm of Divorce*, manila folder, pencil, crayons

- **For the leader:** None

PROCEDURE:

Tell the children that you will be meeting with them nine times to talk about *divorce*. During the meetings, they will have an opportunity to share their feelings about divorce and learn how other children feel about the topic. The children will be compiling a booklet entitled *How I Weathered the Storm of Divorce,* which they will be able to take home to share with their parents after the group meetings have ended.

Have the group members introduce themselves and describe the status of their parents' relationship (separated, filed for divorce, divorced).

Give each child a copy of page 2 of the booklet, a manila folder, a pencil, and crayons. Point to the blank line on the second line of page 2. Have each child write his/her name on the line at the top of the page.

Read page 2 aloud to the group. Ask the children to follow along as you read.

Ask the children:

> "What do you think the word *wisdom* means?" *(Wisdom means becoming more knowledgeable and using this knowledge to make good decisions.)*

Tell the children that, during these group meetings, they will become more knowledgeable about the feelings they have about divorce. This will help them make better decisions about their situations.

Ask the children:

"What were some times when you had to be brave?"

"What did you learn about yourself from these experiences?"

Talk about individual strengths and how they can be used to get through difficult times.

Instruct the children to design the shield on page 2 with symbols and colors that reflect their strengths.

Point out that the picture is of a child who lives in a castle.

Ask the children:

"Who else lives in a castle?"

When the word *knight* is mentioned, steer the discussion in another direction. Explain that knights sought the advice of experienced and wise people to help them in difficult situations.

Ask the children:

"Who, within your family, church, school, or community, can you go to for help in a difficult situation?"

Tell the children to color the page. Tell them how much time they will have to complete the task. When the children have finished coloring, ask them to put the page into their manila folders. Collect the folders, pencils, and crayons.

SUPPLEMENTARY ACTIVITIES:

(To be used if time allows or at a follow-up session.)

Discuss *chivalry*. Emphasize that knights used strength of character and knowledge, as well as physical strength, to overcome difficulties.

Read an appropriate Arthurian story.

⚔ SESSION 2 ⚔

MATERIALS NEEDED:

- **For each child:** Copy of pages 3 and 4 from *How I Weathered the Storm of Divorce*, his/her manila folder from the last session, crayons

- **For the leader:** None

PROCEDURE:

Begin the session by asking the children:

"What does the word *divorce* mean?"

Allow time for answers.

Give each child a copy of pages 3 and 4, his/her manila folder, and crayons.

Read page 3 aloud to the group.

Ask the children:

"What made you think that your parents might separate?"

Allow time for answers. Relate the children's answers to reasons why parents might divorce.

Read page 4 aloud to the group.

Point out the differences between physical and emotional pain. Explain that words do not cause pain unless we think about those words in a way that allows them to upset us. Thinking that way leaves us feeling bad. It is called *negative thinking*.

Ask the children:

"How might the child change his or her thinking to help himself or herself feel better?"

Suggest the use of phrases such as *even if* or *even though* to replace negative phrases such as *what if* and *if only*. Follow these statements with an *I can* or *I know* statement. For example, instead of saying, "What if my mom and dad get divorced? I could stop thinking about it if only I knew they would both still love me." Say, "Even if my mom and dad get divorced, I know they both still love me." Explain that replacing negative thoughts with positive ones is called *positive self-talk*. Make sure the children understand these words as positive self-talk will be referred to in later sessions.

As with any new skill, children are likely to need help in forming these statements until they have practiced saying them several times. Ask the children to state some sentences about themselves and divorce that begin with *what if* and *if only*. Then have them change these sentences into *even if* and *even though* statements. Tell the children to practice using this new skill and to be prepared, at the next session, to tell how they have used it.

Ask the children to think about what both pictures in their booklets mean and then color the pages. Tell them how much time they will have to complete the task. When they have finished coloring the pages, tell the children to put both pages into their manila folders. Collect the manila folders and crayons.

⚔ SESSION 3 ⚔

MATERIALS NEEDED:

- **For each child:** Copy of pages 5 and 6 from *How I Weathered the Storm of Divorce*, his/her manila folder from the last session, pencil, crayons

- **For the leader:** Large sheet of paper, black marker

PROCEDURE:

Begin the session by asking the children:

"Are there any experiences you would like to share with us about when you used *even if* and *even though* statements?"

Allow time for answers.

Give each child a copy of pages 5 and 6, his/her manila folder, a pencil, and crayons.

Read page 5 aloud to the group.

Ask the children:

"Will you share some of the thoughts you had when your parents separated?"

Tell the children to write what they thought about when their parents separated in the cloud on page 5.

Ask the children to remember the skill they learned in the last session. Tell them to restate any negative thoughts in positive self-talk. It is important to point out that although those thinking skills cannot end the separation, they can help ease the emotional pain associated with the situation.

Read page 6 aloud to the group.

Tell the children to complete the face so that its expression shows the way they felt at the time of their parent's separation. Ask the children to write on the banner a list of things that upset them. (Younger children may need help with the writing.) Tell them how much time they will have to complete both tasks.

Ask the children:

"What happened to your family's living arrangement when your parents separated?"

"What changes have occurred in your lives as a result of the separation or divorce?"

"How did these changes make you feel?" *(Sad, angry, afraid.)*

Allow time for answers.

Divide the large sheet of paper into two columns. Title one column "Can Change" and the other "Cannot Change." Ask the children to make a list of things they can change in their lives and a list of things they cannot change.

Ask the children:

"What happens when you try to change something over which you have no control?" *(You get frustrated because you can't do what you want to do.)*

"What is the meaning of the word *frustration*?" *(confusion, inability to understand why what you're doing isn't working)*

Encourage the children to apply their positive self-talk skills to a frustrating situation.

Point out that nobody can change anyone else, and that children cannot change decisions made by adults.

Ask the children:

"Can you tell us how you rely on adults to make important decisions for you?"

Tell the children to color pages 5 and 6. Tell them how much time they will have to complete the task. When the children have finished coloring, ask them to put both pages into their manila folders.

Collect the manila folders, crayons, and pencils.

Encourage the children to continue practicing positive self-talk skills until the next session.

⚔ SESSION 4 ⚔

MATERIALS NEEDED:

- **For each child:** Copy of pages 7 and 8 from *How I Weathered the Storm of Divorce*, his/her manila folder from the last session, pencil, crayons

- **For the leader:** None

PROCEDURE:

Give each child a copy of pages 7 and 8, his/her manila folder, a pencil, and crayons.

Read page 7 aloud to the group.

Ask the children:

"Can you tell us about a time when you were in school and you began to think about the problems you were having at home?"

"Has anyone ever missed hearing the teacher's directions, had trouble completing work, or done poorly on an assignment because of thinking about the divorce?"

Allow time for answers.

Tell the children to look at the bubble on page 7. Tell the children to write in the bubble any thoughts they have had during school time about their problems at home.

Allow sufficient time for the children to share their work with the group and to restate their responses using positive self-talk.

Ask the children:

"What do you do in school to keep your mind off the problems at home?"

Allow time for answers.

Ask the children:

"What does it mean to *worry?* *(To be upset, fret, or feel anxious.)*

"Can worry change anything?" *(No.)*

Tell the children that *worry* is a product of negative thinking. Let the children know that they can talk to a teacher or counselor if their worrying interferes with their concentration in school. Emphasize that parents will worry less and be happier knowing that their children are doing their best in school.

Read page 8 aloud to the group.

Ask the children:

"What different routines, rules, and expectations do you follow in the two households you live?" *(Allow time for answers.)*

"What must you do about these differences, even if you do not think they are fair?" *(Learn to live with them.)*

Review the discussion on frustration from the last session, and apply positive self-talk strategies to situations the children feel are unfair. For example, "If only my mom would let me stay up as late as my dad does, I could see the TV programs I want," is negative thinking. Positive self-talk is, "Even though I can't stay up as late at Mom's as at Dad's, I can still see most of the programs I like."

Help the children discover that each person is responsible for his/her own happiness. Encourage the children to develop self-reliance by asking themselves, "Am I doing what I need to be doing?" when they feel life is not fair.

Explain to the children that accepting things they feel are unfair will often open the door to appropriate compromises in unfair situations.

Tell the children to color pages 7 and 8. Remind them to add, on page 8, a picture of something they left at one of their homes. Tell them to put their finished pages into their folders. Tell them how much time they will have to complete the task. Collect the manila folders, crayons, and pencils.

✠ SESSION 5 ✠

MATERIALS NEEDED:

- **For each child:** Copy of pages 9 and 10 from *How I Weathered the Storm of Divorce*, his/her manila folder from the last session, pencil, crayons

- **For the leader:** None

PROCEDURE:

Give each child a copy of pages 9 and 10, his/her manila folder, a pencil, and crayons.

Read page 9 aloud to the group.

Ask the children:

"What are some of the things that have happened since your parents separation when your parents have been in the same place or talked on the telephone."

Allow time for answers.

Emphasize that children have no control over the emotions and actions of adults. Explain that adults involved in a divorce may, just as children do, experience feelings of anger, fear, and sadness.

Tell each child to think of a time when he/she did something out of anger and without thinking. Explain to the children that feelings do not happen as quickly as lightning strikes and that practicing positive self-talk can help keep anger under control. Emphasize that it is difficult to make good choices when you are upset.

Stress the importance of staying out of the way if adults are involved in a physical confrontation.

Ask the children:

"If your parents are angry with each other and they begin hurting each other, what can you do to keep yourself safe, and how can you get help?"

Allow time for answers. Review when and how to call the local emergency services numbers (911, etc.).

(Leader's note: Not all children will be or have been brought into court for divorce proceedings, but many of them will be familiar with the vocabulary of divorce.)

Ask the children:

"How many of you have been to court?"

"What happened when you were there?"

Read page 10 aloud to the group.

Ask the children:

"What do you think the word *custody* means?" *(The person who has custody of you is the person you live with and who takes care of you.)*

"What feeling do you get when you hear the word *custody?" (Allow time for answers.)*

Have the children use the positive self-talk strategies to restate any negative responses.

Invite the children to ask questions about any divorce-related words that are unfamiliar or unclear to them.

Tell the children to finish the face on page 10 giving it an expression that shows how they believe the child feels about custody. Then, have the children write on the banner the name of the person or persons who have custody of them. Tell the children to color pages 9 and 10. Tell them how much time they will have to complete the tasks.

When the children have finished coloring, ask them to put the pages into their manila folders. Collect the manila folders, crayons, and pencils.

Remind the children to practice using positive self-talk until the next meeting.

⚜ SESSION 6 ⚜

MATERIALS NEEDED:

- **For each child:** Copy of page 11 from *How I Weathered the Storm of Divorce*, his/her manila folder from the last session, pencil, crayons

- **For the leader:** None

PROCEDURE:

Begin the session by asking the children to describe any situations in which they used positive self-talk.

Give each child a copy of page 11, his/her manila folder, a pencil, and crayons.

Ask the children:

"What do you think *stress* means?" (Continue accepting answers until the word *pressure* is mentioned.)

Then allow the children to tell what pressures they have that cause them to feel stress.

Ask the children:

"Have you ever noticed how problems you have forgotten during the day have a way of popping into your mind at bedtime?"

Allow time for answers. Emphasize that stressful things are sometimes responsible for making it hard to sleep.

Read page 11 aloud to the group. Have the children write in the bubble something that they might think about that would keep them from sleeping. Tell them how much time they will have to complete the task. When the children have finished, have them share their responses with the group.

Ask the children:

"What can you do to get to sleep when troubling thoughts keep you awake?"

Allow time for answers. Encourage the children to use positive self-talk and quiet activities such as reading, listening to soft music, or drawing before going to bed.

Ask the children:

"What does it mean to *blame* somebody for something?"

"Why do people try to blame someone other than themselves?" *(Sometimes people feel more in control of and less responsible for an unpleasant situation if somebody or something else can be blamed for it.)*

Explain that children may feel confused about who is to blame for the divorce and may blame themselves, their parents, or an outsider for their circumstances.

Ask the children:

"Are children responsible for the decisions adults make?" *(No.)*

"Will finding fault with either parent change anything?" *(No.)*

Tell the children to think about what was said earlier about stress.

Ask the children:

"Can stress affect the way people behave toward one another?" *(Yes.)*

"Can you tell us about a time when you misbehaved because of the anger you felt toward your mother, your father, or yourself?"

Explain that when these times occur, children can handle their anger by using positive self-talk, becoming interested in something else, or getting involved in a physical activity.

Tell the children to color page 11. Tell them how much time they will have to complete the task. When the children have finished coloring, ask them to put the page into their manila folders. Collect the manila folders, crayons, and pencils.

⚔ SESSION 7 ⚔

MATERIALS NEEDED:

- **For each child:** Copy of pages 12 and 13 from *How I Weathered the Storm of Divorce*, his/her manila folder from the last session, pencil, crayons

- **For the leader:** 3 candles, matches

PROCEDURE:

Give each student a copy of pages 12 and 13, his/her manila folder, a pencil, and crayons.

Begin the session by asking the children:

"Have any of you ever felt you had to choose sides in the divorce or that you could/should love only one of your parents?"

"Why do you think children might feel this way?"

Allow time for answers.

Read page 12 aloud to the group.

Emphasize that parents have disagreements over many things. Because children are one of parents' biggest responsibilities and concerns, they are likely to disagree about many things that involve children. Emphasize that it is not the child's fault that his/her parents argue. Tell the children to circle the things on page 12 their parents have fought about.

Tell the children that when their parents argue, they should talk to themselves, using the positive self-talk strategies they have learned. For example, when they hear their parents arguing about their schoolwork, children should *not* say to themselves, "I really must be dumb. I can't please them." They *should* say, "Even if they are arguing about my schoolwork, I know that I am trying to do my best."

Explain that there is unlimited room in every heart to love and care for others. Use the following candle activity to demonstrate this. Light one candle. Tell the children that the flame on the candle represents the love they have in their hearts. Using the first candle, light the second candle. Tell the children that the second candle represents the love that they have in their hearts for their mothers.

Ask the children:

"Has the flame on your candle gotten any smaller because you gave some of your love away?" *(No.)*

Then use the first candle to light the third candle. Tell the children that this candle represents their fathers.

Ask the children:

"Has the flame on your candle gotten any smaller because you gave some of your love away?" *(No.)*

Repeat that there is unlimited room in every heart to love and care for others.

Read page 13 aloud to the group.

Ask the children:

"Have you ever been so overwhelmed by the changes divorce has brought in your life that you feel like the child in this picture?"

"What are some of the reasons you have felt that way?"

"What do you do when things seem hopeless?"

Review the lesson on blame.

Ask the children:

"Why do children sometimes decide their parents' divorce is their own fault?"

Tell the children that often children upset themselves by thinking they should be able to change things they cannot change. When they do this, they sometimes feel afraid, guilty, and even angry. These feelings are unreasonable, and children should use positive self-talk when they find themselves making unreasonable demands on themselves. For example, they could say, "Even though my parents are getting a divorce, I know that it is not my fault. It is between the two of them."

Tell the children to color pages 12 and 13. Tell them how much time they will have to complete the task. When the children have finished coloring, ask them to put both pages into their manila folders. Collect the manila folders, crayons, and pencils.

23

⚔ SESSION 8 ⚔

MATERIALS NEEDED:

- ◉ **For each child:** Copy of pages 14, 15, 16, and 17 from *How I Weathered the Storm of Divorce*, his/her manila folder from the last session, pencil, crayons

- ◉ **For the leader:** None

PROCEDURE:

Give each student a copy of pages 14 -17, his/her manila folder, a pencil, and crayons.

Begin the session by asking the children:

"What does it mean to be perfect?"

"What do you remember from our last meeting, when we talked about what happens when children make unreasonable demands on themselves? " *(They blame themselves for the divorce and then feel afraid, guilty, and angry toward themselves.)*

Allow time for answers.

Read pages 14 and 15 aloud. On page 15, have each of the children draw a picture of a mistake he/she has made. Tell them how much time they will have to complete the task. When the children have finished, ask them to share their pictures with the group and to describe what they thought of themselves when they made the mistake. Point out any negative statements.

Explain that children sometimes tell themselves they are worthless or stupid if they aren't perfect.

Ask the children:

"Why doesn't it make sense to think that way about yourself?" *(No one is perfect.)*

"How could it be harmful to think that way about yourself?" *(You could lose faith in yourself.)*

Tell the children that children often think of ideas that might reunite their parents.

Ask the children:

"What are some of the ideas you have had about getting your parents back together?"

Discuss the reasons why those attempts are likely to fail. Empathize that divorce is a matter over which children have no control.

Read pages 16 and 17 aloud to the group. Ask the children to complete the face on page 17. Tell them how much time they will have to complete the task.

Ask the children:

"What changes in your life have left you feeling sorry for yourself?"

Allow time for answers.

Remind the children what they have learned about stress: that hopeless feelings may cause physical illness, lack of energy, and other serious problems.

Ask the children:

"What do you think about your parents' dating?"

"What do you think about one or both of your parents finding a new family?"

Tell the children that it is normal to feel some kind of loss and even abandonment when a parent becomes involved with someone else, especially if that person has children of his/her own. But even though children may have those feelings, they should not think that their life is miserable.

Ask each child to complete this statement:

"If only _____, I could be happy."

When the children have finished, point out that they cannot expect others, even the people who love them, to be responsible for their feelings. Feelings are unique and personal and the way they deal with their feelings is a choice they must make themselves. That choice can be either positive, which will help them, or negative, which will make them continue to feel bad. Have the children change the *if only* statements they just made into *even though* statements. Point out how the *even though* statement is helpful and the *if only* statement is not.

Tell the children to color their pages. Tell them how much time they will have to complete the task. When the children have finished coloring, ask them to put the pages into their manila folders. Collect the manila folders, crayons, and pencil.

25

⚜ SESSION 9 ⚜

MATERIALS NEEDED:

- ◉ **For each child:** Copy of pages 18, 19, and 20 and the cover (page 1) from *How I Weathered the Storm of Divorce*, his/her manila folder from the last session, pencil, crayons

- ◉ **For the leader:** Stapler and staples

PROCEDURE:

Give each student a copy of pages 1 and 18-20, his/her manila folder, a pencil, and crayons.

Ask the children:

"Did you ever do something that you really were not sure you wanted to do, like giving a speech in front of the class or jumping off a high diving board?"

"Why do you think you did what you did and did not give up?"

"How did you feel after you had done the difficult task?"

Allow time for answers. Tell the children that the things they did were examples of extra determination and courage.

Read pages 18-20 aloud to the group.

Ask the children:

"What does the word *bold* mean? *(daring, brave, courageous)*

"What does the word *wise* mean? *(knowledgeable, learned)*

"What does the word *true* mean?" *(correct, faithful, loyal)*

"How do these words relate to what you have learned in the group?" *(Sometimes, you have to be bold when fighting off the Storm of Divorce by thinking clearly even when everything seems to cloud up your brain; wise to know the real facts and not try to change what you cannot change; and true to yourself, during all of the turmoil, by not blaming yourself for the divorce.)*

Point out that the storm on page 18 is still there, just as the divorce has not gone away. Explain to the children that what they have learned will not eliminate bad times from their lives, but will help them to cope with them more effectively, and be reasonably happy and productive.

Have the children look at the shields they drew on page 2. Tell them to complete the shield on page 19, showing one new strength they have acquired from participating in the group. Tell them how much time they will have to complete the task.

Ask the children to state aloud some words or sentences they could say to make themselves feel better when they are feeling sad, hurt, or confused. When the children have finished, tell them to select one word or sentence and write it on the rainbow on page 20.

Have each child write his/her name on the cover and color pages 1, 18, 19 and 20. Tell them how much time they will have to complete the task. Then take all the pages out of the manila folders and staple them together into a book.

Read the entire book with the group as a closing activity.

Ask the children:

"What would you like to say about what you have learned in this group?"

Allow time for answers. Then thank the children for their participation and cooperation and tell them you are confident they will be using positive self-talk to handle any difficult situations that may arise in the future.

HOW I WEATHERED THE STORM OF DIVORCE

NAME

~ 1 ~

This is my story.
A bold, knightly tale of how I, _____ ,
A kid just like you, Weathered the Divorce Storm,
And in wisdom grew.

Write your name on the line and design your shield.

Color the picture.

~ 2 ~

I first spied those dark clouds
Blocking the sun's light,
When my mother and father
Started to fight.

A fog dimmed my windows
And oozed under my door,
As a bone-chilling draft
Weirdly clung to the floor.

Color the picture.

~ **3** ~

Ooooh! It was awful!
So cold, windy, and bleak!
Alone, scared, and helpless,
I dared not even speak.

Color the picture.

~ 4 ~

Then came the day
That the Storm of Divorce
Entered my home,
Its winds howling full force.

My dad packed his stuff
And he patted my head,
While I held Mother's hand,
My heart full of dread.

In the cloud, write what you thought when your parents separated.

Color the picture.

Gales howled and thunder rolled,
Spitting bolts of blue-white fire,
As my whole life was tossed
Into a sea of murky mire.

Finish the face. List the things that upset you on the banner.

Color the picture.

~ 6 ~

Then there were days
When foul weather would rule,
And the gloom of the squall
Fogged my thinking in school.

Fill the bubble.

Color the picture.

~ 7 ~

My dad lived in one place,
my mom in another.
The storm hovered above me
From one place to the other.

My shoes would be here.
My toys would be there.
I'd forget all my homework!
It just wasn't fair!

Color the picture.

Draw a picture of something you left at one of your homes.

~ 8 ~

One day when my dad
Picked me up to go out,
The Storm's lightning struck Mom,
And she started to shout.

My dad looked up angry,
As bullets of hail fell.
And stung by the ice,
He just started to yell.

I stood there and worried
About what they might do.
I knew I couldn't stop them,
But I felt guilty and blue.

Color the picture.

~ 9 ~

I thought that the Storm
Would never, ever budge,
When I had to go to court
And talk to the judge.

There were lots of new words
That were explained to me.
The one that hurt most
Was the word *custody*.

Write the name or
names of who has
custody of you on
the banner.

Finish the face.

Color the picture.

~ 10 ~

Sometimes in the night,
As I lay in my bed,
Storms of confusion
Would rage in my head.

I felt that I needed
To find someone to blame.
Was it Mom? Was it Dad?
How I hated this game!

So I'd get angry with Dad,
And say things that were bad.
Then I'd stop minding my Mom
So she would feel sad.

Fill in the bubble.

Color the picture.

And as torrents of rainy thoughts
Flooded my brain,
The Storm of Divorce
Caused me still greater pain.

I wondered if my heart
Was so tiny and small
I could just love one parent,
And that was all.

I started to wonder.
Perhaps that was right.
They always did argue
When I was in sight.

They'd yell about money,
How late I stayed up,
About holidays, presents,
My schoolwork, my pup!

Circle the things your parents fight about.

Color the picture.

I felt swallowed up
By a cyclone in a wild, reckless spin.
I was stuck in the middle
Of a game no one could win.

While that dreaded Divorce Storm
Raged all the more,
It gathered up energy
And started to pour.

And so in a deluge
Of anger, guilt, and fear,
The words, "It was my fault"
Seeped into my ear.

I looked at myself,
Thought I was stupid, spoiled, and mean.
And Mom and Dad were fed up
'Cause my room didn't stay clean.

Color the picture.

~ 13 ~

Those awful thoughts really hurt me.
They stung like a bee.
But they gave me new hope
As I thought, "Golly, gee!"

"If I can just get
Mom and Dad back together,
I'll be perfectly perfect
Forever and ever!"

Color the picture.

~ 14 ~

But soon I discovered,
It just wouldn't work.
I tried to be perfect,
But the storm clouds still lurked.

It just didn't matter
How hard I tried.
My heart started breaking.
I cried and I cried.

Draw a picture of a mistake you made. Color the picture.

~ 15 ~

My dad started missing
Our times spent together.
He found a new family
I thought he loved better.

Mom met a man
Who lived in the city.
If she's going to love him,
What will happen to me?

Color the picture.

~ 16 ~

I longed for the day
When my life could be sunny.
I felt sorry for me.
Mom never had any money.

My head ached so badly,
I thought my brain would burst.
My tummy felt crummy,
I couldn't remember feeling worse.

Finish the face. Color the picture.

~ **17** ~

Then came the day
When I'd just had enough!
I faced that Divorce Storm,
Although it was tough.

While fixing my eyes
In the deep gray, dank, haze,
I searched in my heart
For some bright, sunny rays.

Color the picture.

~ 18 ~

My answer came soon
When my eyes did behold
My foul-weather armor
Of glistening, bright gold.

The shield shone so brightly,
It turned gray skies to blue.
Then I spied my glistening lance.
It read, "Wise, Bold, and True."

With lance held skyward,
I spoke from my heart,
And the Storm of Divorce,
Cloud by cloud, fell apart.

Complete the shield.
Color the picture.

~ 19 ~

I can change my feelings
With new kinds of thoughts,
About growing and learning
And how worry blots.

There's fun and good times
That life's meant to hold.
So away with the thunder!
Let the rainbow unfold!

*Write on the rainbow something you
could say to help you feel better.*

Color the picture.

~ 20 ~